JOHN MONTAGUE

A Slow Dance

D1345008

THE DOLMEN PRESS

LONDON: OXFORD UNIVERSITY PRESS
NORTH AMERICA: WAKE FOREST UNIVERSITY PRESS

Set in Pilgrim type and printed and published
in the Republic of Ireland at the Dolmen Press,
North Richmond Industrial Estate,
North Richmond Street, Dublin 1

ISBN 0 85105 283 5 THE DOLMEN PRESS
ISBN 0 19 211857 9 OXFORD UNIVERSITY PRESS
ISBN 0 916390 01 2 WAKE FOREST UNIVERSITY PRESS

First published 1975
in association with Oxford University Press
and Wake Forest University Press

Oxford University Press, Ely House, London W.1
GLASGOW   NEW YORK   TORONTO   MELBOURNE   WELLINGTON
CAPE TOWN   IBADAN   NAIROBI   DAR ES SALAAM   LUSAKA   ADDIS ABABA
DELHI   BOMBAY   CALCUTTA   MADRAS   KARACHI   LAHORE   DACCA
KUALA LUMPUR   SINGAPORE   HONG KONG   TOKYO

Wake Forest University Press
WINSTON-SALEM, NORTH CAROLINA 27109

*

A Slow Dance is a Christmas 1975
Recommendation of the Poetry Book Society.

CONTENTS

I

A SLOW DANCE

I Back *page* 7
II Sweeny 8
III The Dance 9
IV Message 10
V Seskilgreen 11
VI For the Hillmother 12
VII The Hinge Stone & the Crozier 13

II

Sawmill, Limekiln 15
Courtyard in Winter 16
Small Secrets 19
A Song for Synge 21
Homes 22
Dowager 23
Views 24
Almost a Song 25
The Errigal Road 26
Windharp 28

III

THE CAVE OF NIGHT

I Underside 29
II The Plain of Adoration 29
III Cave 30
IV All Night 31

v   Falls Funeral 32
vi   Ratonnade 33

Killing the Pig 34

Hero's Portion 36
Heroics 38
Wheels Slowly Turning 39

COLDNESS

i   Northern 41
ii   The Massacre 41
iii   Border Lake 42
iv   Northern Express 42

IV

A Muddy Cup 44
Mother Cat 46
A Graveyard in Queens 48
At Last 51
All Souls 52
Colonel, Retreating 53
Shadow 56

V

Ó RIADA'S FAREWELL

i-iv   Woodtown Manor, Again 57
v   Samhain 59
vi   Hell Fire Club 60
vii   The Two Gifts 61
viii   Lament 63

I

A SLOW DANCE

I : BACK

Darkness, cave
drip, earth womb

we move slowly
back to our origins

the naked salute
to the sun disc

the obeisance
to the antlered tree

the lonely dance
on the grass

earth darkness
clouded moon

whirling arms
they shuffle

hair flying
eyes flashing

instep echoing
one, two as

bare heels, toe
smite the earth

II : SWEENY

A wet silence.
Wait under trees,
muscles tense,
ear lifted, eye alert.

Lungs clear.
A nest of senses
stirring awake —
human beast !

A bird lights :
two claw prints.
Two leaves shift :
a small wind.

Beneath, white
rush of current,
stone chattering
between high banks.

Occasional shrill
of a bird, squirrel
trampolining along
a springy branch.

Start a slow
dance, lifting
a foot, planting
a heel to celebrate

greenness, rain
spatter on skin,
the humid pull
of the earth.

The whole world
turning in wet
and silence, a
damp mill wheel.

III : THE DANCE

In silence and isolation, the dance begins. No one is
meant to watch, least of all yourself. Hands fall to
the sides, the head lolls, empty, a broken stalk. The
shoes fall away from the feet, the clothes peel away
from the skin, body rags. The sight has slowly faded
from your eyes, that sight of habit which sees nothing.
Your ears buzz a little before they retreat to where
the heart pulses, a soft drum. Then the dance begins,
cleansing, healing. Through the bare forehead, along
the bones of the feet, the earth begins to speak. One
knee lifts rustily, then the other. Totally absent, you
shuffle up and down, the purse of your loins striking
against your thighs, sperm and urine oozing down
your lower body like a gum. From where the legs join
the rhythm spreads upwards — the branch of the penis
lifting, the cage of the ribs whistling — to pass down
the arms like electricity along a wire. On the skin
moisture forms, a wet leaf or a windbreath light as a
mayfly. In wet and darkness you are reborn, the rain
falling on your face as it would on a mossy tree trunk,
wet hair clinging to your skull like bark, your breath
mingling with the exhalations of the earth, that eternal
smell of humus and mould.

IV : MESSAGE

With a body
heavy as earth
she begins to speak;

her words
are dew, bright
deadly to drink

her hair
the damp mare's
nest of the grass

her arms,
thighs, chance
of a swaying branch

her secret
message, shaped
by a wandering wind

puts the eye
of reason out;
so novice, blind,

ease your
hand into the
rot smelling crotch

of a hollow
tree, and find
two pebbles of quartz

protected by
a spider's web:
her sunless breasts.

V : SESKILGREEN

A circle of stones
surviving behind a
guttery farmhouse,

the capstone phallic
in a thistly meadow :
Seskilgreen Passage Grave.

Cup, circle,
triangle beating
their secret dance

(eyes, breasts,
thighs of a still
fragrant goddess).

I came last in May
to find the mound
drowned in bluebells

with a fearless wren
hoarding speckled eggs
in a stony crevice

while cattle
swayed sleepily
under low branches

lashing the ropes
of their tails
across the centuries.

Hinge of silence
           creak for us
Rose of darkness
           unfold for us
Wood anemone
           sway for us
Blue harebell
           bend to us
Moist fern
           unfurl for us
Springy moss
           uphold us
Branch of pleasure
           lean on us
Leaves of delight
           murmur for us
Odorous wood
           breathe on us
Evening dews
           pearl for us
Freshet of ease
           flow for us
Secret waterfall
           pour for us
Hidden cleft
           speak to us
Portal of delight
           inflame us
Hill of motherhood
           wait for us
Gate of birth
           open for us

VII : THE HINGE STONE AND THE CROZIER

1
Praise the stone :
flying from Wales,
its blue grain grows light as a feather !

Pour the libation !
The tame serpent glides to the altar
to lap the warm spiced milk.

2
As the first ray
of the midsummer sun
strikes through the arches

the seething scales
around the astronomer's neck
harden to the coils of a torque.

3
His vestments
stiff with the dried blood
of the victim, old Tallcrook advances

singing & swaying
his staff, which shrivels & curls :
a serpent ascending a cross.

II

SAWMILL, LIMEKILN

On the way to Geneva
the streams ran down
the side of the road
the deep, light sound
of water over rock
following us to the saw-
mill where we tried
to sleep on pine chips
pricklier than straw,
a plank harder than
stone, mountain air
colder than ice.

II
The collapsing stone
of the lime-kiln was
where the polly cow
sheltered to have her
calf, in the open.
When I couldn't find
her that evening,
I came out again
just after dawn
to find her licking it
clean and delivered
— already standing up.

COURTYARD IN WINTER

Snow curls in on the cold wind.

Slowly, I push back the door.
After long absence, old habits
Are painfully revived, those disciplines
Which enable us to survive,
To keep a minimal fury alive
While flake by faltering flake

Snow curls in on the cold wind.

Along the courtyard, the boss
Of each cobblestone is rimmed
In white, with winter's weight
Pressing, like a silver shield,
On all the small plots of earth,
Inert in their living death as

Snow curls in on the cold wind.

Seized in a giant fist of frost,
The grounded planes at London Airport,
Mallarme swans, trapped in ice.
The friend whom I have just left
Will be dead, a year from now
Through her own fault, while

Snow curls in on the cold wind.

Or smothered by some glacial truth?
Thirty years ago, I learnt to reach
Across the rusting hoops of steel
That bound our greening waterbarrel
To save the living water beneath
The hardening crust of ice, before

Snow curls in on the cold wind.

But despair has a deeper crust.
In all our hours together, I never
Managed to ease the single hurt
That edged her towards her death;
Never reached through her loneliness
To save a trust, chilled after

Snow curls in on the cold wind.

I plunged through snowdrifts once,
Above our home, to carry
A telegram to a mountain farm.
Fearful but inviting, they waved me
To warm myself at the flaring
Hearth before I faced again where

Snow curls in on the cold wind.

The news I brought was sadness.
In a far city, someone of their name
Lay dying. The tracks of foxes,
Wild birds as I climbed down
Seemed to form a secret writing
Minute and frail as life when

Snow curls in on the cold wind.

Sometimes, I know that message.
There is a disease called snow-sickness;
The glare from the bright god,
The earth's reply. As if that
Ceaseless, glittering light was
All the truth we'd left after

Snow curls in on the cold wind.

So, before dawn, comfort fails.
I imagine her end, in some sad
Bedsitting room, the steady hiss
Of the gas more welcome than an
Act of friendship, the protective
Oblivion of a lover's caress if

Snow curls in on the cold wind.

In the canyon of the street
The dark snowclouds hesitate,
Turning to slush almost before
They cross the taut canvas of
The street stalls, the bustle
Of a sweeper's brush after

Snow curls in on the cold wind.

The walls are spectral, white.
All the trees black-ribbed, bare.
Only veins of ivy, the sturdy
Laurel with its waxen leaves,
Its scant red berries, survive
To form a winter wreath as

Snow curls in on the cold wind.

*

What solace but endurance, kindness?
Against her choice, I still affirm
That nothing dies, that even from
Such bitter failure memory grows;
The snowflake's structure, fragile
But intricate as the rose when

Snow curls in on the cold wind.

SMALL SECRETS

Where I work
out of doors
children come
to present me
with an acorn
a pine cone —
small secrets —

and a fat
grass snail
who uncoils
to carry his
whorled house
over the top
of my table.

With a pencil
I nudge him
back into
himself, but
fluid horns
unfurl, damp
tentacles, to

probe, test
space before
he drags his
habitation
forward again
on his single
muscular foot

rippling along
its liquid self-
creating path.
With absorbed,
animal faces
the children
watch us both

but he will
have none of
me, the static
angular world
of books, papers —
which is neither
green nor moist —

only to climb
around, over
as with rest-
less glistening
energy, he races
at full tilt
over the ledge

onto the grass.
All I am left
with is, between
pine cone & acorn

the silver smear
of his progress
which will soon

wear off, like
the silvery galaxies,
mother of pearl
motorways, woven
across the grass
each morning by
the tireless snails

of the world,
minute as grains
of rice, gross
as conch or
triton, bequeath-
ing their shells
to the earth.

A SONG FOR SYNGE

Deep glens of silence
upper levels of feathery
changing cloud lower levels
of light as through an open
window streaming!

                    A horse
canters past the small lake
halts, hoofs abruptly earthed
in aftergrass.

What holds his rigid eyeball?

A complaint of ewes upon
a snail wet mountain path;
the noiseless violent slide
of a waterfall?

                    Creation bright
each object shines & stirs like
the dark waves the swaying
pine crests & the mind
turns again on its root
back into the secret shell
of loneliness.

HOMES

I: FAMINE COTTAGE

Soft flute note of absence;
Above MacCrystal's glen
Where shaggy gold of whin
Overhangs a hidden stream
I stumble upon a cabin,
Four crumbling walls and
A door, a shape easily
Rising from the ground,
As easily settling back:
Stones swathed in grass.

Tennysonian solitudes of cliff
and waterfall —
silent, driving rain
clearing as sudden as it falls.
At the far end of the lake
a hunting lodge.
The black hoods of the carriages
outside the hall door
are spattered with rain.

DOWAGER

I dwell in this leaky Western castle.
American matrons weave across the carpet,
Sorefooted as camels, and less useful.

Smooth Ionic columns hold up a roof.
A chandelier shines on a foxhound's coat:
The grandson of a grandmother I reared.

In the old days I read or embroidered,
But now it is enough to see the sky change,
Clouds extend or smother a mountain's shape.

Wet afternoons I ride in the Rolls;
Windshield wipers flail helpless against the rain:
I thrash through pools like smashing panes of glass.

And the light afterwards! Hedges steam,
I ride through a damp tunnel of sweetness,
The bonnet strewn with bridal hawthorn

From which a silver lady leaps, always young.
Alone, I hum with satisfaction in the sun,
An old bitch, with a warm mouthful of game.

VIEWS

I : BACK DOOR

Oh, the wet melancholy
of morning fields! We
wake to a silence more
heavy than twilight
where an old car finds
its last life as a henhouse
then falls apart slowly
before our eyes, dwindling
to a rust-gnawed fender
where a moulting hen
sits, one eye unlidding;
a mystic of vacancy.

II : KERRY

Shapes of pine and cypress
shade the hollow where
on thundery nights
facing uphill, the
cattle sleep. Blossoms
of fuchsia and yellow whin
drift slowly down upon
their fragrant, cumbersome
backs. Saga queens,
they sigh, knees
hidden in a carpet
of gold, flecked with
blue and scarlet.

ALMOST A SONG

Early summer, the upper bog,
slicing the thick, black turf,
spreading, footing, castling
and clamping, ritual skills
ruled by the sun's slow wheel
towards Knockmany, save when
a dark threat or spit of rain
raced us to shelter under
a tunnel damp corner
of the bank.
        At mealtimes
huge hobnails sparkled
a circle in the stiff grass
as we drank brown tea, bit
buttered planks of soda bread;
a messenger first, then helper,
I earned my right to sit among
the men for a stretch & smoke
while we put our heads together
in idle talk of neighbours
and weather.
        Almost a song
as we gathered ourselves again
and the flies spindled all
afternoon over the lukewarm
oily depths of the boghole
before we called quitting
time, stowed the flanged
spade, the squat turf barrow,
& tramped down the mountain
side, the sun over Knockmany,
old Eagleson leading, home.

1964

THE ERRIGAL ROAD

We match paces along the Hill Head Road,
the road to the old churchyard of Errigal Keerogue;
its early cross, a heavy stone hidden in grass.

As we climb, my old Protestant neighbour
signals landmarks along his well trodden path,
some hill or valley celebrated in local myth.

'Yonder's Whiskey Hollow', he declares,
indicating a line of lunar birches.
We halt to imagine men plotting

against the wind, feeding the fire or
smothering the fumes of an old fashioned worm
while the secret liquid bubbles & clears.

'And that's Foxhole Brae under there —'
pointing to the torn face of a quarry.
'It used to be crawling with them.'

(A red quarry slinks through the heather,
a movement swift as a bird's, melting as rain,
glimpsed behind a mound, disappears again.)

At Fairy Thorn Height the view fans out,
ruck and rise to where, swathed in mist
& rain, swells the mysterious saddle shape

of Knockmany Hill, its brooding tumulus
opening perspectives beyond our Christian myth.
'On a clear day you can see far into Monaghan,'

old Eagleson says, and we exchange sad notes
about the violence plaguing these parts;
last week, a gun battle outside Aughnacloy,

machine gun fire splintering the wet thorns,
two men beaten up near dark Altamuskin,
an attempt to blow up Omagh Courthouse.

Helicopters overhead, hovering locusts.
Heavily booted soldiers probing vehicles, streets,
their strange antennae bristling, like insects.

At his lane's end, he turns to face me.
'Tell them down South that old neighbours
can still speak to each other around here'

& gives me his hand, but does not ask me in.
Rain misting my coat, I turn back towards
the main road, where cars whip smartly past

between small farms, fading back into forest.
Soon all our shared landscape will be effaced,
a quick stubble of pine recovering most.

WINDHARP
for Patrick Collins

The sounds of Ireland,
that restless whispering
you never get away
from, seeping out of
low bushes and grass,
heatherbells and fern,
wrinkling bog pools,
scraping tree branches,
light hunting cloud,
sound hounding sight,
a hand ceaselessly
combing and stroking
the landscape, till
the valley gleams
like the pile upon
a mountain pony's coat.

III

THE CAVE OF NIGHT
for Sean Lucy

> *Men who believe in absurdities*
> *will commit atrocities.*
>
> Voltaire

I: UNDERSIDE

I have seen the high
vapour trails of the last
destroyers in dream :
I have seen the grey
underside of the moon
slide closer to earth . . .

II: THE PLAIN OF ADORATION
   from the Irish, eleventh century

Here was raised
a tall idol of savage fights :
the Cromm Cruaich —
the King Idol of Erin.

He was their Moloch,
this withered hump of mists,
hulking over every path,
refusing the eternal kingdom.

In a circle stood
four times three idols of stone :
to bitterly enslave his people,
the pivot figure was of gold.

In dark November,
when the two worlds near each other,
he glittered among his subjects,
blood-crusted, insatiable.

To him, without glory,
would they sacrifice their first-born :
with wailing and danger
pouring fresh blood for the Stooped One.

Under his shadow
they cried and mutilated their bodies :
from this worship of dolour
it is called the Plain of Adoration.

Well born Gaels lay prostrate
beneath his crooked shape until
gross and glittering as a cinema organ
he sank back into his earth.

III : CAVE

The rifled honeycomb
of the high-rise hotel
where a wind tunnel moans.
While jungleclad troops
ransack the Falls, race
through huddled streets,
we lie awake, the wide
window washed with rain,
your oval face, and tide
of yellow hair luminous
as you turn to me again
seeking refuge as the
cave of night blooms
with fresh explosions.

All night spider webs
of nothing. Condemned to
that treadmill of helplessness.
Distended, drowning fish,
frogs with lions' jaws.
A woman breasted butterfly
copulates with a dying bat.
A pomegranate bursts slowly
between her ladyship's legs.
Her young peep out
with bared teeth :
the eggs of hell
fertilizing the abyss.

Frail skyscrapers incline
together like stilts.
Grain elevators melt.
Cities subside as liners
leave by themselves
all radios playing.
A friendly hand places
a warm bomb under
the community centre
where the last evacuees
are trying a hymn.
Still singing, they
part for limbo, still
tucking their blankets
over separating limbs.

A land I did not seek
to enter. Pure terror.

Ice floes sail past
grandly as battleships.
Blue gashed arctic distances
ache the retina and
the silence grows to
a sparkle of starlight —
sharpened knives.
Lift up your telescope,
old colonel, and learn
to lurch with the penguins!
In the final place
a solitary being begins
its slow dance. . . .

V : FALLS FUNERAL

Unmarked faces
fierce with grief

a line of children
led by a small coffin

the young
mourning the young

a sight beyond tears
beyond pious belief

David's brethren
in the Land of Goliath.

Godoi, godoi, godoi!
Our city burns & so did Troy,
Finic, Finic, marshbirds cry
As bricks assemble a new toy.

    Godoi, godoi, godoi.

Humble mousewives crouch in caves,
Monster rats lash their tails,
Cheese grows scarce in Kingdom Come,
Rodents leap to sound of drum.

    Godoi, *etc.*

Civilisation slips & slides when
Death sails past with ballroom glide:
Tangomaster of the skulls whose
Harvest lies in griefs & rues.

    Godoi, *etc.*

On small hillsides darkens fire,
Wheel goes up, forgetting tyre,
Grudgery holds its winter court,
Smash and smithereens to report.

    Godoi, *etc.*

Against such horrors hold a cry,
Sweetness mothers us to die,
Wisens digs its garden patch,
Silence lifts a silver latch.

    Godoi, *etc.*

Mingle musk love-birds say,
Honey-hiving all the day,
Ears & lips & private parts,
Muffled as the sound of carts.

Godoi, *etc*.

Moral is of worsens hours,
Cripple twisting only flowers,
One arm lost, one leg found,
Sad men fall on common ground.

Godoi!

KILLING THE PIG

The noise.

He was pulled out, squealing,
an iron cleek sunk in the roof
of his mouth.

(Don't say they are not intelligent :
they know the hour has come
and they want none of it;
they dig in their little trotters,
will not go dumb or singing
to the slaughter.)

That high pitched final effort,
no single sound could match it —

a big plane roaring off,
a *diva* soaring towards her last note,
the brain-chilling persistence of an electric saw,
scrap being crushed.

Piercing & absolute,
only high heaven ignores it.

Then a full stop.
An expert plants
a solid thump of a mallet
flat between the ears.

Swiftly the knife seeks the throat;
swiftly the other cleavers work
till the carcass is hung up
shining and eviscerated as
a surgeon's coat.

A child is given
the bladder to play with.
But the walls of the farmyard
still hold that scream,
are built around it.

HERO'S PORTION

When dining they all sit not on chairs, but on the ground, strewing beneath them wolf- or dog-skins. . . . Beside them are the hearths blazing with fire, with cauldrons and spits with great pieces of meat; brave warriors are honoured by the finest portions.

Diodorus Siculus

I

A steaming hunk of meat
landed before him —

it was red & running
with blood & his stomach

rose & fell to see it
his juices churned to meet it
his jaws opened to chew it

cracking & splitting down
to the marrow stuffed bone
which he licked & sucked

as clean as a whistle

before he sighed 'Enough!'
and raised his gold ringed arms

to summon one
of the waiting women
to squat across his lap

36

while the musician pulled
his long curved nails
through the golden hair
of his harp.

II

What song to sing?
the blind man said :

sing the hero
who lost his head

sing the hero
who lopped it off

sing the torso
still propped aloft

sing the nobles
who judged that fall

sing the sword
so fierce & tall

sing the ladies
whose bowels crave

its double edge
of birth & grave.

III

Timbers creak
in the banquet hall;
the harper's fingers
are ringed with blood
& the ornate battle sword
sheathed in its scabbard.
The king has fallen asleep
under the weight of his crown
while in the corner a hound
& bitch are quarrelling
over the hero's bone.

HEROICS

In an odour of wet hawthorn
arm-swinging heroes march,
eyes chill with yearning.
They sport dark berets and
shoulder rifles as forthrightly
as spades. Spider webs
lace their sparbled boots.
A burst of automatic fire
solves the historical problem.
They drop to one knee.

WHEELS SLOWLY TURNING

Seen, school years ago,
on a summer morning
an army lorry
like a beetle
upsidedown in a ditch
wheels slowly turning

*

we worked all day
clearing the battlefield
hosing down the corpses
loading them onto the trucks
the padre ran out of holy water
we ran out of strength

*

off duty, tired & smelly
as in a slaughter yard
bridegrooms of death
swathed in her filth
'knee-deep in knight's blood,
hip-deep in the blood of heroes.'

*

Her love-making
is like a skirmish
a litany of boots,
catalogued limbs, uniforms
a harvest necklace of heads,
a wedding girdle of arms

*

Black widow goddess
she believes in war
watches the battalions
step crisply out
to topple in a valley
a crushed centipede

*

Envoi

Huzza, you cried, seeing a leg
leap into the air, like a hat,
a baseball or cricket bat
hurled high after a home run,
a long drawn but winning game

& then you realised it was your own
and sat down
awkwardly
sideways, to cry
among the other dying men

which you did not, and now
wooden-legged, piratical,
you thump around your Paris flat to tell
how many toothsome ladies fell
for your game leg

'they beg
to handle it', you say,
and wake to find it dangling
— a hunter's weapon —
around their bedpost
at peep of day.

COLDNESS

I : NORTHERN

Thick and vertical
the glacier slowly
a green white wall
grinding mountains
scooping hollows
a gross carapace
sliding down the
face of Europe
to seep, to sink
its melting weight
into chilly seas;
bequeathing us
ridges of stone,
rubble of gravel,
eskers of hardness :
always within us —
a memory of coldness.

II : THE MASSACRE

Two crows flap to a winter wood.
Soldiers with lances and swords
Probe the entrails of innocents.
A burgomeister washes manicured
Hands before mourning citizens.
The snow on the gable is linen crisp,
That on the ground laced with blood.
Two crows flap to a winter wood.

41

III : BORDER LAKE

The farther North you travel, the colder it gets.
Take that border county of which no one speaks.
Look at the straggly length of its capital town :
the bleakness after a fair, cattle beaten home.
The only beauty nearby is a small glacial lake
sheltering between drumlin moons of mountains.
In winter it is completely frozen over, reeds
bayonet sharp, under a low, comfortless sky.
Near the middle, there is a sluggish channel
where a stray current tugs to free itself.
The solitary pair of swans who haunt the lake
have found it out, and come zigzagging
holding their breasts aloof from the jagged
edges of large pale mirrors of ice.

IV : NORTHERN EXPRESS

Before Aughnacloy, they are ordered to dismount.
For God and Ulster, he shouts, waving a pistol,
a shadow in the twilight, daft as Don Quixote,
except for that gun, stuck in the driver's throat
and brother shadow, sullen in his trenchcoat.
A forced companionship of passengers tremble
by the sleety roadside, attending sudden death.
Assistant shadow sprinkles petrol leisurely
over the back and sides of the Derry express
while chief shadow asks them to remove their boots,
the classic ritual before a mass execution.
Lucky this time, they are spared, warned off
to march behind the driver two miles in the snow
not daring, like Lot's wife, to look for the glow
of their former bus, warming the hedges :
their only casualty, thin socks soaked through.

42

IV

Fusillade of raindrops.
I fall asleep in the room
where my father was born.
Ghosts buffet the walls
creak lovingly as I dream.
I haul them up, one by one,
from the well of darkness,
greet and name each face —
warm playing cards.

A MUDDY CUP
A Ballad of Brooklyn,
for Charley Monaghan

My mother
my mother's memories
of America;
a muddy cup
she refused to drink

his landlady didn't know
my father was married
so who was the woman
landed on the doorstep
with growing sons

my elder brothers
lonely & lost
Father staggered back
from the speak-easy
for his stage entrance

(the whole scene as
played by Boucicault
or Eugene O'Neill :
the shattering of
that early dream)

but that didn't
lessen the anguish
soften the pain so
she laid into him
with the frying pan

and harshly under
a crumbling brownstone
roof in Brooklyn
to the clatter of
garbage cans

like a loving man
my father leant
on the joystick
& they were reconciled
made another child

a third son who
beats out this song
to celebrate the odours
that bubbled up
so rank & strong

from that muddy cup
my mother refused
to drink but kept
wrinkling her nose
in souvenir of

(cops & coppers
cigar store Indians
& coal black niggers
bathtub gin &
Jewish neighbours)

years after
she had returned
to the hilly town
where she had
been born

a she cat,
intent on safety,
dragging her kittens
to the womb-warm basket
of home.

MOTHER CAT

The mother cat
opens her claws
like petals

bends her spine
to expose her
battery of tits

where her young
toothless snouts
screwed eyes

on which light
cuffs mild
paternal blows

jostle & cry
for position
except one

so boneless
& frail it
pulls down

air, not milk.
Wan little scut
you are already

set for death
never getting
a say against

the warm circle
of your mother's
breast, as she

arches voluptuously
in the pleasure
of giving life

to those who
claim it, bit-
ten navel cords

barely dried,
already fierce
at the trough.

A GRAVEYARD IN QUEENS
for Eileen Carney

We hesitate along
flower encumbered

avenues of the dead;
Greek, Puerto-Rican,

Italian, Irish —
(our true Catholic

world, a graveyard)
but a squirrel

dances us to it
through the water

sprinklered grass,
collapsing wreaths,

& taller than you
by half, lately from

that hidden village
where you were born

I sway with you
in a sad, awkward

dance of pain
over the grave of

my uncle & namesake—
the country fiddler—

& the grave of almost
all your life held,

your husband & son
all three sheltering

under the same
squat, grey stone.

*

You would cry out
against what has

happened, such
heedless hurt,

had you the harsh
nature for it

48

(swelling the North
wind with groans,

curses, imprecations
against heaven's will)

but your mind is
a humble house, a

soft light burning
beneath the holy

picture, the image
of the seven times

wounded heart of
her, whose portion

is to endure. For
there is no end

to pain, nor of
love to match it

& I remember Anne
meekest of my aunts

rocking & praying
in her empty room.

Oh, the absurdity
of grief in that

doll's house, all
the chair legs sawn

to nurse dead children :
love's museum!

*

It sent me down
to the millstream

to spy upon a
mournful waterhen

shushing her young
along the autumn

flood, as seriously
as a policeman and

after scampering
along, the proud

plumed squirrel
now halts, to stand

at the border
of this grave plot

serious, still,
a small ornament

holding something
a nut, a leaf —

like an offering
inside its paws.

*

For an instant
you smile to see

his antics, then
bend to tidy

flowers, gravel
like any woman

making a bed,
arranging a room,

over what were
your darlings' heads

and far from
our supposed home

I submit again
to stare soberly

at my own name
cut on a gravestone

& hear the creak
of a ghostly fiddle

filter through
American earth

the slow pride
of a lament.

AT LAST

A small sad man with a hat
he came through the customs at Cobh
carrying a roped suitcase and
something in me began to contract

but also to expand. We stood,
his grown sons, seeking for words
which under the clouding mist
turn to clumsy, laughing gestures.

At the mouth of the harbour lay
the squat shape of the liner
hooting farewell, with the waves
striking against Spike Island's grey.

We drove across Ireland that day,
lush river valleys of Cork, russet
of the Central Plain, landscapes
exotic to us Northerners, halting

only in a snug beyond Athlone
to hear a broadcast I had done.
How strange in that cramped room
the disembodied voice, the silence

after, as we looked at each other!
Slowly our eyes managed recognition.
'Well done' he said, raising his glass:
father and son at ease, at last.

ALL SOULS

All the family are together.
A yellow glass of whiskey punch in one hand
John Joe is rehearsing his oldest joke;
He whinnies into laughter a head
Before the others.

His bald spot glistens
And the pates of half of those listening,
Eager to assist out his say, to get
Their own oar in —

human warmth!
The details of the room hardly matter,
The stuffed cock pheasant, the photo
Of Uncle James at the World's Fair,
Three smiling nuns. That polite, parlour
Coldness, stale air, and dying armchairs.
And the dusty silence of the piano lid
Which has not been lifted since Auntie died:
An ebony glitter.

God rest her,
A dead hand runs down the scales,
Diminuendo. And Uncle James wanders in,
Tapping the hall barometer with his fingernail,
Fussily, before he appears,

a decent skeleton.

II

Now the dead and their descendants
Share in the necessary feast of blood.
A child's voice trembles into song,
A warm sphere suspended in light.
The knuckles lifting the clove scented glass
To your lips are also branched with bone
So toast your kin in the chill oblong
Of the gilt mirror where the plumage
Of a shot bird still swells chestnut brown.

COLONEL, RETREATING

After breakfast, he retired
into his brown study.

Sometimes I tiptoed in.
He sat at a rolltop desk

not noticing his daughter's
head at the height of his elbow.

He never looked up
but little boxes slid in, out

a pen stood upright in an inkwell
a paperweight held down a cloud of papers.

*

After lunch he slept, a handkerchief
sheeted over mouth and nose
while the house breathed around him,
wooden panelled, odorous,
small snores breaking like bubbles
from his drowning solitude.

*

Before dinner, a last turn.

Half a century before, heavily horsed
he flourished a sabre to rally troops
and plunge across the Somme.

Now he parades the lawn
inspecting rosebushes, a hexagon
of laurel, correcting a corner
where a spider works to join
a branch & a wall, with classic
curled moustache & military carriage,
matching his energy against the dying sun.

And, after the dinner gong,
what a ransacking of bones,
a reaching out of large hands,
a sucking of moustache ends!
On his plate rose a mountain-
slide of gristle and rinds,
morsels shrinking as teeth
grind, in rhythm.

*

Yet pity the heart locked in,
too human proud to speak,
too animal strong to break.
Mouse quiet in the night,
I heard the floorboards creak
as, cloudhuge in his nightgown,
he prowled the house, halting
only when, gnawed by the worm
of consciousness, disappointment
at disappointment, he stood
on the porch to inhale
the hay and thistle scented
air of a Normandy harvest;
piss copiously in salutation
towards a shining moon.

*

Sound retreat after
disorder's final victory.
He charged his car
straight into an oak.

The day of his funeral
the gravediggers struck.
He was carried by lunatics
who let the coffin lurch.
Cannon heavy, it vaulted
upsidedown into the earth.

SHADOW

I

Asleep, like a month old child,
Young Matthew, who took a plane
One morning to Tokyo, another night
Flew to Majorca, mission impossible
To locate a pal in Palma, phoning:
Leave a light on, I'll know your hut.
Now propped asleep in his chair,
Pale, fair hair like ripening wheat,
Throttle open in his dreaming cot:
One hundred & thirty on the straight.
Pubs and clubs and changing girls,
Another frothing round of champagne
After the races, wallet thinning but
Still coming up again; we hope.

II

And still a sense of loneliness abides.
At night, on the long country roads,
Car beams cross, like the waverings
Of some primaeval intelligence.
We rush past each other into darkness,
Eased only by the feelers of another,
Approaching from a far hill: and then
The car's outline rides the hedge again,
A shadow keeping company with itself.
Once I remember brakes slamming, and
Something caught between my wheels,
Like a hurt animal, and then screaming,
And then stop. If I can keep moving
Fast enough, the shadow may not catch up.

V

Ó RIADA'S FAREWELL

'To have gathered from the air a live tradition.'

Ezra Pound

Roving, unsatisfied ghost,
old friend, lean closer;
leave us your skills :
lie still in the quiet
of your chosen earth.

WOODTOWN MANOR, AGAIN

I

We vigil by the dying fire,
talk stilled for once,
foil clash of rivalry,
fierce Samurai pretence.

Outside a rustle of bramble,
jack fox around the framing
elegance of a friend's house
we both choose to love :

two natives warming ourselves
at the revived fire
in a high ceilinged room
worthy of Carolan —

clatter of harpsichord
the music leaping
like a long candle flame
to light ancestral faces

pride of music
pride of race

II

Abruptly, closer to self-revelation
than I have ever seen, you speak;
bubbles of unhappiness breaking
the bright surface of *Till Eulenspiegel*.

I am in great danger, you whisper,
as much to the failing fire
as to your friend & listener;
though, *you have great luck*.

Our roles reversed, myself cast
as the light-fingered master,
the lucky dancer on thin ice,
rope walker on his precipice.

III

I sense the magisterial strain
behind your jay's laugh,
ruddy moustached, smiling,
your sharp player's mask.

Instinct wrung and run
awry all day, powers idled
to self-defeat, the vacuum
behind the catalyst's gift.

Beyond the flourish
of personality, peacock
pride of music or language :
a constant, piercing torment!

Signs earlier, a stranger
made to stumble at a bar door,
fatal confusion of the powers
of the upper and lower air.

A playing with fire, leading
you, finally, tempting you
to a malevolence, the
calling of death for another.

IV

A door opens,
and she steps into the room,
smothered in a black gown,
harsh black hair falling to her knees,
a pale tearstained face.

How pretty you look,
Miss Death !

V : SAMHAIN

Sing a song
for the mistress
of the bones

the player
on the black keys
the darker harmonies

light jig
of shoe buckles
on a coffin lid

*

pale glint
of the wrecker's lantern
on a jagged cliff

across the ceaseless
glitter of the spume :
a seagull's creak.

the damp haired
seaweed stained sorceress
marshlight of defeat

*

chill of winter
a slowly failing fire
faltering desire

Darkness of Darkness
we meet on our way
in loneliness

Blind Carolan
Blind Raftery
Blind Tadgh

VI: HELL FIRE CLUB

Around the house all night
dark music of the underworld,
hyena howl of the unsatisfied,
latch creak, shutter sigh,
the groan and lash of trees,
a cloud upon the moon.

Released demons moan.
A monstrous black tom
couchant on the roofbeam.
The widowed peacock screams
knowing the fox's tooth:
a cry, like rending silk

& a smell of carrion where
baulked of their prey,
from pane to tall window
pane, they flit, howling
to where he lies, who has
called them from defeat.

Now, their luckless meat,
turning a white pillowed room,
smooth as a bridal suite
into a hospital bed where
a lucid beast fights against
a blithely summoned doom.

At the eye of the storm
a central calm, where
tearstained, a girl child
sleeps cradled in my arms
till the morning points
and you are gone.

VII: THE TWO GIFTS

And a nation mourns:
The blind horseman with his harp carrying servant,
Hurrying through darkness to a great house
Where a lordly welcome waits, as here:

Fingernail spikes in candlelight recall
A ripple & rush of upland streams,
The slant of rain on void eye sockets,
The shrill of snipe over mountains
Where a few stragglers nest in bracken —
After Kinsale, after Limerick, after Aughrim,
After another defeat, to be redeemed
By the curlew sorrow of an aisling.

> *The little Black Rose*
> *(To be sprinkled with tears)*
> *The Silk of the Kine*
> *(To be shipped as dead meat)*

> *'They tore out my tongue*
> *So I grew another one',*
> *I heard a severed head*
> *Sing down a bloody stream.*

But a lonelier lady mourns,
the muse of a man's particular gift,
Mozart's impossible marriage of fire & ice,
skull sweetness of the last quartets,
Mahler's horn wakening the autumn forest,
the harsh blood pulse of Stravinsky,
the hammer of Boulez
                        which you will never lift.

Never to be named with your peers,
I am in great danger, he said;
firecastles of flame,
a name extinguished.

VIII: LAMENT

With no family
& no country

a voice rises
out of the threatened beat
of the heart & the brain cells

(not for the broken people
nor for the blood soaked earth)

a voice
like an animal howling
to itself on a hillside
in the empty church of the world

a lament so total
it mourns no one
but the globe itself
turning in the endless halls

of space, populated
with passionless stars

and that always raised voice

Macedonia 1972 — Cork 1974

ACKNOWLEDGEMENTS

Acknowledgements are due to the editors of the following, where some of these poems first appeared : *Acorn, Antaeus, Aquarius, Critical Quarterly, Exile, Esquire, Hibernia, The Honest Ulsterman, Icarus, The Irish Press, The Irish Times, Irish University Review, Lines, The Nation, The New Review, The New Statesman, New Poems 1972-3,* The Poem of the Month Club, *Poetry Now* (BBC), *Soundings, St. Stephen's, The Tablet, The Times Literary Supplement.*

'Message' was first published as a poster poem by the Arts Council of Northern Ireland, with artwork by Brian Ballard. 'The Cave of Night' and 'O Riada's Farewell' were the first two publications of the Golden Stone, 25 Grattan Hill, Cork. 'Wheels Slowly Turning' is indebted to the memories of a medical orderly friend of mine, who helped to clear many battlefields. 'O Riada's Farewell' is called after my friend's last record, for which I helped to choose the title (Claddagh Records).